Previously on Stream of Consciousness:
Submerged

Thought Twenty: P.O.W.

I had a dream.
Of all dreams, I had a bad one.
Everything I desired was within my grasp.
Finances were a concern of the past.
Food was in bulk.
Clothes were of the latest fashion.
I had the house that the eight-year-old me promised my mama.
I had the car every street kid longed for.
That is one thing Martin Luther never told me could occur.
I guess he considered it a detail of minor status.
Because, of all dreams, I had a bad one.
Everything I desired was within my grasp.
I had watches that I threw into foreign territory.
I had shoes that cost the souls of two creatures.
I had employment that left me a servant to no man.
An appeal that appealed to anyone's interest.

I had a dream.
Of all dreams, I had a bad one.
I had everything that was thought worth having.
Except someone to share it with.
Which would have made me happy.

Threw Watches

Thought Twenty-Nine: The Balance

You can lose yourself in the work. I get that some things are time sensitive. Then again, what is time? You are so indulged that you become unproductive. On the road to finding balance. If you have insight, feel free to message me.

10.22.17, Forgot to Set Alarm

Thought Thirty-One: Roses

The sun won't rise always.
May seem farther when it's near.
You can wait until dying days,
Or you can give them roses while they're here.

10.25.17, 1:23 am

Thought Forty-Four: Conversation About Death

"I could die tomorrow. You never know."

"Why do you have to bring up death? I hate when you talk like that."

"You hate when I tell the truth? You do realize that you are going to die one day, right?"

"I know, but I do not like talking about death. It scares me."

"At one point in time, you were scared to talk to me. Now we talk every day. Applying the same logic, maybe if we talked about death more you would not be so scared."

"What if I am still scared to talk to you…"

Death Knows No Time

Thought Forty-Seven: Sleepless Nights

A series that is long overdue. The territory of time where I could have documented my most authentic self throughout the years. The transitional period between consciousness and death, before I am expected to resurrect in four hours for a day long shift of telling kids to follow their dreams. In these moments, the streams truly flow endlessly. The thoughts branch out into various directions.

I anticipate the immediate work ahead that I am too lazy to work on at this time. I imagine my future. Do I want a wife or kids? I said I never wanted any, but what if? Should I move across the country and learn a new language in the process? What would people think of me? Would the kids think I abandoned them? I should have played sports in high school. Had I known I would be 6'3... Finishing the book. What am I going to wear tomorrow?

Healthcare.

I will stop typing now…

"Time keeps slippin' away"

I was drowning.

The abrasive currents of the stream rushed mercilessly. The might of every droplet forced me beneath the surface. I couldn't breathe. Though submerged within the stream, I was conscious of the tears that flowed down. I couldn't breathe. I desperately flailed my helpless arms, hoping to rise to get at least one final breath of air. Water consumed me, filling every crevice of my lungs. I couldn't breathe.

I was drowning. It felt like there wasn't anyone there to save me.

I realized that when you're drowning, you desperately reach to grab anything that makes you feel secure. I was willing to latch on to the support of a serpent, sure that it was better than allowing my lifeless body to aimlessly drift with the ruthless flow of the stream. I was drowning. In those moments, I have the tendency to grasp onto anything that is offered. I reached my hand to the serpent, only to have two forceful palms clenched around my collar. In my moment of vulnerability, I reached out for support. As a result, I earned a counteracting force that thrusted me deeper into the bed of my pitiless stream of thought.

I was drowning. It felt like there wasn't anyone there to save me.

Stream of Consciousness:
Hoodie Season

Derick Stephenson Jr.

"Jermaine's Interlude" by DJ Khaled ft. J. Cole

Copyright © 2019 by Derick L. Stephenson Jr.

All rights reserved. No part of this publication may be reproduced, distributed, or transmitted in any form or by any means, including photocopying, recording, or other electronic or mechanical methods, without the prior written permission of the publisher, except in the case of brief quotations embodied in critical reviews, and certain other noncommercial uses permitted by copyright law. If you have read this far, then you are one of very few people who read cover to cover. It is appreciated. So much goes into mapping out every word. I am thankful that you are taking the time to hear my story. I love you.

First printing 2019, Kindle Direct Publishing.

Cover designed by Cody Davis.
Contact: codydavisdesign@gmail.com

ISBN-13: 978-1-7326043-1-5

What is this?

This is a playlist.
This is a journal for your thoughts.
This is creative expression.

This is a product of a challenge that I pushed myself to write. For some of the content, I chose to make extensions to pieces that already existed. Otherwise, the bulk of this material was developed within *twenty-four hours*. There is music attached to each thought. For some, these are the songs that I listened to on repeat as I developed the thought. Overall, these are songs that I feel may connect with each piece. Additionally, there are videos attached to provide context and commentary. You should be able to pull up the videos using your smartphone camera. If that does not work, download a QR code scanner in order to access the videos from the book.

How I desire you to interact with this collection?

Spend time alone with this one. While reading this, there is nowhere else that you need to be. There is no rush. Cut off the distractions. Turn up the AC. **Put on your favorite hoodie.** Spend time writing your own thoughts.

Feel free to share your thoughts with me.
Much love.

Welcome to Hoodie Season

We must make a conscious decision of what we dedicate our being toward. What woke you up this morning? What is going to keep you up tonight? What is going to push you to fight past the tears, pain, and time?

What is your dedication?

_____

"Dedication" by Nipsey Hussle ft. Kendrick

Stream of Consciousness:
"A person's thoughts and conscious reactions to events, perceived as a continuous flow."

I value writing and reflection. I want to offer you the opportunity to document your thoughts. I am open to feedback and criticism in these journal sections. Feel free to use these pages to share your thoughts.

What are your thoughts before reading?

Now I lay me down to sleep

Thought: Dreams and Nightmares

If I ever need a solid intro, I would put my money on Meek.

Got me thinking about my dreams. Dreams turning into my nightmares. Everything I ran toward flipping into the fears I run from. The things I stand for being the cause of my fall. The rise is my demise.

Most would attest, as a kid I was quiet. I cannot paint the picture that I was not annoying and did not disturb the peace. However, I learned that my most intimate thoughts should be reserved for me. Even then, I dreamed. I dreamed of being on stage speaking in front of thousands. I wanted to get to that platform without being a politician. I am not a rapper. I do not like being labeled a poet. I dreamed of being a man who lived his life with purpose. I do not know why I am speaking as if these are dreams of the past. Every night, I visualize myself pouring my heart out to the crowds.

You.
I want you to laugh for me.
I want you to cry for me.

I know how that goes. I have not felt it for myself, but I have witnessed it one too many times. Kendrick said it best: "How many leaders you said you needed then left them for dead?"

I feel like I do not deserve to have that fear. For what? What have I done but cower away from attention to any issue worth mention? Yet, it is still there. The idea that one day I will be a voice for the masses. Only to meet the day that the masses do not love me anymore. All I have sacrificed will not mean the same anymore.

You.
You will not scream my name anymore.

Meek got me thinking. I am writing this like: "They gon' remember me."

"Dreams and Nightmares" by Meek Mill

Thought: The In Between

Bruh, I have been feeling like a bum. Really been feeling down and out. Lost track of time for a second.

Missing showers.

Missing meals.

Same shirt for three days.

Locked myself in a room.

Just me and my thoughts.

Thinking until I forget to think.

Remembering until I forget what I thought.

All because I do not have a job.

I must laugh out loud on that one. Since when did I allow my self-worth to be determined by my employment status? It has been feeling like I am stepping into these interviews giving all the honor to institutions for the opportunity. I was fooling myself by thinking that I do not have anything meaningful to offer. I was foolish to think that I am not an asset. I stopped and reflected on my value being beyond the figures on a paycheck. Just as your worth is more than the things that you own.

Yes, you.
You are more than the cars, clothes, and money. You are more than what you know and who you know. You are more than how you look. You are something the world has never seen.

Do not forget that.

"I Am Not My Hair" by India Arie

Thought: Stay Afloat

As much as I want to take credit for the things I have achieved, I recognize that I would not be anything without others who have poured into me.

For a minute now, my ears have consumed the voices of celebrities and public figures who proclaim to be self-made. I, like many others, have regarded these people with high esteem. However, no longer can I put another being on a pedestal. Except Will Smith. You know, because Will Smith is Will Smith.

No one is self-made. Many hands are in the bowl working to sculpt us into who we are. I cannot undermine the individual effort. There are things that people do not see:
The three in the morning sessions, being sleep deprived and hyped off whatever keeps you energized, or trying to balance between your future, family, friends, and foes.

I get it. I cannot discredit the life that anyone else is living. What I know is, I would not be here without the care and generosity of other people. I remember the days when we did not have anything but a pitcher of water in the refrigerator. I had a teacher named Ms. Rains who went out of her way to buy groceries for my family. I think about the hands that stitched together the fabric on my feet. I am thankful for the people who pointed out the potential in me.
Folks asked me why I included footnotes about others in my first book. I did it because I cannot climb the ladder without bringing up others who have helped me along the way.

The time will come when I am able to put on for the people who have helped me stay afloat.

"Bigger Than Me" by Big Sean

Thought: Broken Mirror

I was told to stay faithful to the people that I've been with.
People looked at you and said I was a spittin' image.
The truth:
When I think about you,
I'm taken back to grass roots.
The proof:
Second grade picture day we're both snaggletooth.

'Til this moment still, I know you hate to hear it.
Being face to face with you was like lookin' in the mirror.
It's not that you don't love me.
We're brothers.
But at times we can see the world differently.
You knew how the streets could be.
You didn't want what you been through to hurt the people that you've been with.

But 'til this moment still,
When I picture you, I picture myself.
Young poor blacks
Developing schemes to accumulate wealth.
Praised if we grow through the concrete,
But no one questions who let us slip through the cracks.

A chance you took.
You couldn't see your path was crooked.
I begged you to change,
But you pitied poor people who had to beg for change.

Just like you,
A chance, I took.
I just felt better off puttin' my money on books.

Years later, you hit my line, I'm puttin' my money on books.

I'll do it Every. Single. Time.
No questions asked.

Because I was told to stay faithful to the people that I've been with.

Even though I hate that I have to talk to you through this hole in the glass every time I visit.
You used to be my muse.
Now you're the root of my misery.
You tell me that you're missin' me.
We're separated because we're seein' pens differently.
You're in the penitentiary.
Sent you copies of my books just to show you what pens did for me.

'Til this moment still,
When I picture you, I picture myself.
You're chained by shackles.
I'm chained by survivor's guilt.

'Til this moment still,
I know you hate to hear it.

Being face to face with you is like lookin' into a broken mirror.

"Three Wishes" by J. Cole

Thought: Explanation for Cain

The text message read:

> You said this on Saturday. You also said it when you came back from Cali. I asked you about your trip. "I probably won't go into that level of detail with anybody else." Unpack that in your writing. I thought that was a very interesting statement that could definitely be elaborated. Exposed. A sharing point.

Explanation: In short, I know people do not care.
I have been in a mode of trying to practice transparency.
Transparently, I know that there are many communicative exchanges that people would rather not engage in. The only reason why people entertain them is because societal norms make us feel obligated. How many times have you asked someone how they are doing out of courtesy rather than genuine inquiry? How many times have you been asked, only to offer a half-hearted response?

If you ask me about my experience, I would much rather question the degree to which you care than to offer more information than what was desired.
There is also an aspect of preservation of self.
I value my privacy.
Like many others, I discovered a good helping of rumors about me that contained no merit. Imagine if I relinquished information that added fuel to that fire. At a certain point in time, I grew exhausted of allowing people to have pieces of me to do with as they please.

My privacy is a protection of me.

"Say What's Real" by Drake

What are your thoughts?

_____
_____
_____
_____
_____
_____
_____
_____
_____
_____
_____
_____
_____
_____
_____
_____
_____
_____
_____
_____
_____
_____
_____

I pray to the Lord my soul to keep

Thought: Justice for My Jerry

I would be lying if I said that we were the best of friends.
If we were, then he deserved way better than me.
Now I am stuck with that hindsight guilt. The thoughts of what I
would do differently if my homie was still alive.

I know we all have our flaws, but Jerry was literally one of the most
beautiful people that I have ever met. He had the voice of an angel.
He emitted vibrations that touched the soul.

It is not an exaggeration. Year after year, I spent time just rereading
every message that he sent. I question whether they ever found his
killer. If not, I question if they are still looking. Makes me question
what would happen if his killer was found and convicted. Would we
call it justice? Brought me to this conclusion: "The only true justice
is prevention." Say they are convicted. That is just another soul
locked up in the system. Another soul taken away from a network of
people that are going to miss them. It will not remove the pain that
stains the heart of every person attached. It will not loosen the
reinforced fears of black men not making it to the milestone of
twenty-five. I have never heard of uncried tears. At the end of the
day, it will not bring Jerry back.

In that Rubik's cube of repercussion, where is the justice?

"Flying Without Wings" by Ruben Studdard
"Uncried Tears" by Ian Manuel (Poem)

Thought: It's My Birthday

Such a disheartening day.

April 6, 2019 to be specific.
It was everything I ever dreamed of.
I felt like God was really looking out for ya boy. Hazardous weather conditions resulted in the rescheduling of the Dreamville Festival. It was only right that I spent my twenty-fifth birthday in the presence of my favorite rapper, J. Cole. That bonus hit my account just in time for me to be able to purchase tickets for my siblings as well.

Such a disheartening day.

It was everything I ever dreamed of.
I was ecstatic. I had never been to a festival before. I did not know what to expect. I really did not know festival etiquette. I should have known it would be crowded and lack any form of personal space. I guess I could have guessed that the beer would be expensive. I did not know that the muddy field would ruin my Jordan ones. However, I was with the ones I love, so it was all worth it. Besides, none of that would matter once Cole hit the stage.

Something that I dreamed about for days had come to fruition. I had a vision that he would call me to the stage for a birthday recognition. I would be able to give him a signed copy of my book that I brought for him. Maybe, just maybe, he would even let me spit my poem "My Therapist."

Such a disheartening day.

It was everything I ever dreamed of.
Even though nothing I envision ever happened, I still jumped around and sung the lyrics. The music was electrifying. I felt blessed and highly favored that I was alive another year to hear it.
It was everything I ever dreamed of.
It was such a disheartening day.

Her name is… was,
Nusrat Jahan Rafi.
She was only nineteen.
Went to school in Bangladesh.
The very school where she filed a complaint against her headmaster.
Eleven days after,
April 6, 2019 to be specific,
Nusrat Jahan Rafi was doused with kerosene.
She was set on fire.
It was reported that doctors found burns covering eighty percent of her body.
All because she spoke up against an injustice.
I think it is evident how this is relevant. Someone asked me what keeps me up at night. Consequently, it is the same thing that prevents me from fully embracing what is supposed to be the joys of life. Juxtapose those two stories and you will witness the illness of the world that we live in. The unfortunate matter is that so many congruent wicked actions transpired on the same day, and the world will never know the other victims' name. Here I am jumping and singing to music that is meaningless when compared to the evil that exists. I am celebrating life, while others are senselessly departing with the world.

This one is for Nusrat Jahan Rafi, and all the voices that are never heard.

"Have Mercy" by Eryn Allen Kane

Thought: Learning to Let Go

I think of it as softening the blow, Sock'em Boppers style. If I am going to be dealt a blow, I would rather have a little padding. Back when my cousins and I used to play wrestle, we would lay pillow cushions out on the floor. We would really stand on top of the arm of the couch and throw each other from, what I now realize was, eight feet in the air. Once in a while, someone would miss the pillow, leading their head to make direct impact with the floor.

As I sit here and chuckle about all the untreated concussions we probably had, I recognize that once we hit our head enough, we became hesitant to climb on that couch again. Eventually, we just stopped playing altogether.

I think this part of my life is called "Learning to Let Go."

Here is what I know. This is not my first or last time in this space. I just feel that I have not always addressed it the right way.

I have noticed that I tend to sabotage. In moments where I feel that I am losing something or someone that I love, I attempt to sabotage the connection before we meet our end.

I have been thinking to myself about what that sabotage looks like. I think I would phrase it as pushing people away.

- Saying hurtful things
- Starting arguments
- Ignoring phone calls/texts
- Declining outings
- Short responses
- Overall distancing myself

The people closest to me know that one of my biggest forms of self-care is questioning myself. I have genuine conversations with my inner being in an effort to be a better self. For so long, I avoided this conversation. I avoided questioning my inclination to sabotage relationships.

I think I create scenarios that contribute to a self-fulfilling prophecy. I think I justify my lack of feeling when I am able to disconnect myself prior to the end of a relationship.

I think I work to save face. I think in certain regards, I work to avoid looking like "the bad guy." I think if I elicit an argument that leads to the finality of the relationship, I leave ownership of the termination on the other being. I think when the more aroused emotions are on the front burner, my true feelings never have to be exposed.

I do not know why I am saying "I think."

In those moments, without recognizing it then, I hurt so many people and cut off numerous opportunities. I hurt so many people because I had a fear of letting go. I hurt so many people, because I feared losing control. I hurt so many people, because of the feelings that I did not want to show. Years later, I acknowledge that I was the root of insecurity for many people that I encountered. People have poured out their heart and tears, while questioning whether they were good enough.

They blamed themselves for what I could not be.
When in truth, the cliché existed:
It was not them; it was me.

My only nemesis is the unpredictability of death.

"Mirror" by Madison Ryann Ward

Thought: Wither Away

These thorns,
They've evolved.
Stemming from the insecurities that I've allowed others to cause.
Those that treated me as a decorative accessory.
Clipped.
On display.
Confined within a vase,
Until my petals wither away.
Only to be replaced.

These thorns,
They've evolved.
Not to be confused as a weapon against the one meant to reap the harvest.
Rather, protection from those who admire
But limit what I have to offer.

What must I do for you to sense this is a cry for love?

I grew these thorns
And learned to be alone
Until I've found what I've been searching for.

A ray of light that shines in the darkest days.
A consistent love despite the season change.
Creative catalyst who
Beholds my beauty before my bud blooms in the spring.
A love that stays when my leaves fall in the autumn.
Affection that feels like the comfort of warm rain.
Eases pain.
Wipes tears.
Erases fears.

A love that recognizes my worth.
A love that loves even when it hurts.
A love that is a haven for my heart as it heals.
A love that doesn't tell me what it is,
But shows me how it feels.

What must I do for you to sense this is a cry for love?

I grew these thorns
And learned to be alone
Until I've found what I've been searching for.

Someone who soothes my soul.
A love deeply rooted enough to withstand the storms.
A love that watches me grow,
Rather than someone who watches me

Wither away.

"Wither Away" by Liesl Michelle

Thought: What I Never Knew About Butterflies.

Quite often, we refer to the change that a caterpillar makes in order to become a butterfly. We talk about the process that it has to endure and the challenges that it has to face. We use the metamorphosis as a metaphorical representation of us becoming our best self. We marvel at the beauty that the butterfly can achieve. We suggest how the challenges endured throughout the process were worth the final outcome.

Today, I learned something about butterflies that I never knew. I was told that, though some may live for months, various factors lead to most butterflies surviving for about two weeks.

All the glory bestowed upon survivors of the hardship, only to be fulfilled for what is a considerably short time period. I search for balance when considering this perspective. Optimism versus being pessimistic. I question the caterpillars view on a life worth living.

Literally, while I am sitting in this Arizona Butterfly Wonderland exhibit:

Random stranger: Is this where you find the solitude, bruh?
Me: Yea, man.
Him: You write music?
Me: Nah, poetry.
Him: Keep doing it. I ain't even heard it. I just know sometimes people don't believe. So, keep doing.
Me: I appreciate that.

Just like that, whatever this butterfly questioned about a life worth living,

I just found my answer.

"Mortal Man" by Kendrick Lamar

Thought: Man in the Mirror

Quite a few times, I have shared my experience with one of the most life-changing activities that I have ever participated in.

I was preparing to facilitate a summer leadership academy. I considered what it would look like to engage the kids in an activity involving self-esteem. I thought of a mirror; the reflection of how one sees themselves.

I engage myself in every single activity that I ask my kids to participate in. I was dating a young lady at the time and invited her to participate as well. The agreement was, each morning for a week, we would stand alone in the mirror and positively affirm ourselves.

Day one, I stood facing the mirror.
Alone.
I wanted to. I really did.
There were countless things that I wanted to express to myself.

I stood facing the mirror.
Though alone, I heard voices. Some that sounded like others. Some that sounded like mine.
Voices that contradicted every positive affirmation that came to mind.

Voices that reminded me of every denial.
Voices that pointed out every imperfection in my smile.
Voices that reminded me of things people said about my voice.
Voices that told me they wish I would have died that night.
Voices that reminded me that I am alone.

Day one, I stood facing the mirror.
Alone.
I told myself that I was worthy of being loved.

"Cranes in the Sky" by Solange

Thought: Cra ZYX

So many people go around parading tales of their crazy ex. Seems boastful at times. Almost as if they want to pride themselves on the indignity of the narratives expressed about their past relations.
So many people go around parading tales of their crazy ex. I get it. For the most part, at least. Who am I to discredit their personal experience? I know there are folks out there with bad intentions. The person they show on the surface is not who they are at heart. They have skeletons concealed in the dark. What fuels their ambitions is their ability to tear you apart. I get it. For the most part, at least.
Used.
Beaten.
Mistreated.
Taken for granted.
The list is more extensive than what I can capture in a one page thought piece.
So many people go around parading tales of their crazy ex.
They have every right to do so. I guess.
Here is one thing I do know.
Not all of your exes were crazy.

Maybe it is just me. Maybe I should be thankful that I do not have an ex that I would portray in that light. As I have grown, I processed the factors that contributed to the downfall of my relationships. Before I ever part my lips to call any of my exes crazy, I must be willing to acknowledge any actions of mine that caused them to display the characteristics that I depict as "crazy." I cannot act like my actions were not the root of insecurities that caused tension between them and me.

A notion that serves as an extension of that is the fact that we all have baggage that others do not always have the strength to carry. I think about anxiety. Anxiety is real. Anxiety displays symptoms that are commonly misconstrued by those who never had to grapple with effects that anxiety can have on an individual. Supporting someone with anxiety may not be a walk in the park but having anxiety does not make a person crazy. Likewise, you are not a bad person if you are not able to manage the responsibility of providing support. It is very much possible that you are not equipped with the tools necessary to address their needs. That is okay to acknowledge. That is just one example. Each former couple has their own narrative. For some of you, I am here to change the narrative. "Crazy" is a heavy title to carry, especially over misunderstandings.

Since each of my break ups, my relationship with exes have not been the same. I know a large factor is me. However, even if that is the case, I could never speak down on their names.

I hope the feelings are mutual.

"Grow'n Pains" by Jon Echols

Thought: The More You Know

Knowing.

It can be devastating to realize how much you do not know.

I am sitting around the table, glad to be seated.

The conversation topic is equity.

I am devastated by how much more others know than me.

I excuse myself.

Sit by the still waters.

It talks to me.

"Though you do not know as much, you have something that they need."

"What is that?" I ask.

"You, my friend, would know that more than me."

"River" by Leon Bridges

Thought: Real Men Wear Pink

"Ain't nothing wrong with my pink. I wear pink. Ain't nothing wrong with my masculinity."

I wondered what would happen if I were to ask that same man his sentiments about wearing rainbow colors. You know, if colors do not dictate your masculinity.

Bruh, over the summer, I experienced the joy of getting a pedicure for the first time in my life. I am twenty-five.

Bruh, for so long, I deprived myself of experiences in the name of masculinity.

I could not dance.

I could not listen to City Girls.

I could not feel the joy of crying.

I could not get a pedicure.

Imagine what it would have looked like if I advanced on the opportunity to go to the nail salon with one of my former girlfriends. I think about how easily that could have been a bonding experience that changed the course of our relationship. I imagine what life would have been like if it had been a part of my self-care regimen years ago. How much stress I would have let go with each rotation of the massaging chair soothing my back.

How much of your happiness have you sacrificed in the name of masculinity?

"Take Yo Man" by City Girls
"Cry" by Lyfe Jennings

What are your thoughts?

If I should die before I wake

Thought: You Have a Friend in Me

I hear it all too often.
Some variation of the question:
If you knew what day you would die, what would you do?
If you knew you would die in the next *twenty-four hours*, how would you spend your time?

We glorify the life changes that folk make after near death experiences. How many movies feature a protagonist who gets a second chance at life? How often do we see folks find their claim to fame and freedom after being diagnosed with a terminal illness, clawing at the hems of Father Time for any ounce of spare change that can be offered?

That last line made more sense in hindsight, only after someone told me that the real currency is time. A social construct in itself. Infinite, though we never seem to have enough. We spend our lives waiting for the right time, only to be dissatisfied with the time we have left. Though not tangible, the only measure of our living is how we choose to spend it.

That is just it. I do not want to wait until my final hours to see the value in the air that I breathe. I do not want to be knocking on death's door when I finally decide to pursue a life that is worth living. Especially considering, my friend always calls me up when I am least expecting.

Death.
Death is my friend.

"If Tomorrow Never Comes" by Lyfe Jennings
"Is There More" by Drake

Thought: Dreams Worth More than Money

I remember my days as a kid.
Youthful days were everlasting, it seemed.
I remember I was always reminded to dream.
In my youthful days, that is exactly what I did.

I remember dreams of being a Power Ranger.
I truly thought I could fly.
I had no wary of potential danger.
I had no concept of what it meant to die.

Until I took that leap off the edge.
On life, it left a permanent stain.
I fell down and broke my leg.
Since then, I have not dreamt the same.

"Dollar and A Dream" III by J. Cole

Thought: Namesake

I question, from whom did I derive my name
Versus, who sculpted me 'til birth?
Answers that do not weigh the same
When explaining my existence on Earth.

Hence, the issue with society:
The senseless attributions to men.
The palm of masculine notoriety
Is not the sole tool for life to begin.

Rather, it is the pot, spoon, baker's batter,
The heat, the pressure, and mother's glance,
The caution, cooling, and patience after
Along, willingness to give life a chance.

The privilege of men to take title and glory
Over a history of creation embedded in her story.

"To Zion" by Lauryn Hill ft. Carlos Santana

Thought: Mary An

Hands of my broken wristwatch
Is set to the expiration date of my Grandfather's clock.
He told me the good die young.
My time is ticking.
Premonitions of my past transgressions returning to get me.
Before I depart,
Echoes repetitively, redundantly, reminding me
That the baker's business is to bake.
Long after their cup has spilled
It is the creator's creation that will be savored most.

My quest has reached a quarter century.
I'm plagued by curiosity, questioning, and intrusive inquiry.
Most regarding the timeline in which I'll marry an honorable lady.

Marianne, you're wrong.

My deepest fear
Is the hurt that I'll project on the ones I'm near.
The truth she'll seek
Will jeopardize the security of the secrets I keep.
My deepest fear
Is that my daughter's father will fail
To Hyder her from the wicked words the world will call her.
My deepest fear
Is that my sun won't have the opportunity to shine its brightest.
The darkness of tomorrow's evil
Will reverse its desire to live.
Rather than shine its rays,
The transgressions of its
Father's past will leave it left astray.
My deepest fear

Is that if I marry an honorable lady,
I'll leave her alone to repair the hand of a broken wristwatch.

But, just as nature's tick continues to tock,
With surety,
I'm told an honorable lady will come along to make my time stop.

Just watch.

"The River by Noel" Gourdin
"Loved by You" by Kirby
"One Man Band" by Old Dominion

Thought: Profound Gentlemen

Many men, freed of expectations
Of who they are supposed to be.
Many men, with stories more profound
Than what eyes can see.

"Black Boy Joy" by Rob LaRay

Thought: Tea from the Top

A dear friend of mine recently lost his mother. Seeing him at his rock bottom reminded me of something his mom once said to me: "Sometimes you have to drink your tea from the top." Being real, I had no idea what she meant. I was just going to accept the statement as a universal truth, similar to all the other ambiguous bits of wisdom that the seasoned folk like to impart on the young and naive. She acknowledged that people have a tendency to sink their straws to the bottom of the cup. However, the tea at the top, where the ice leisurely lingers, is where the tea is the coldest and most refreshing. I never thought about that. Some may think that it is not that deep. Well, I think that is exactly how she intended it to be. I think she meant that sometimes the surface level is okay. As a matter of fact, we often move so fast that we forget to appreciate the small things in life. I remember the first time that one of my parents needed to use their hands while driving and asked me to hold the wheel to keep the car steady. I remember the days of skipping class just to lay out in the grass each spring, allowing the wind to blow through every crevice of my body that was exposed. When I was younger, I was told that the rain was God's tears. During downpours, my sister and I would run out in the rain and splash around in puddles, getting drenched in God's sorrows. How often do you experience jubilation in the rain, recognizing that it is a vital aspect of our human well-being? When is the last time you have screamed at the top of your lungs just because you have a voice? When is the last time that you have danced in the living room in your underwear with Whitney Houston's "I Wanna Dance with Somebody" blasting in the background? Laughed with a baby? Wrote without editing? Called to say hello with no other notion of how the convo will evolve?

This is for me. Sometimes I get caught up.

"Sunday Candy" by Donnie Trumpet & the Social Experiment
"I Wanna Dance with Somebody" by Whitney Houston

Thought: Hoodie Season

My attention ignored the black figure approaching in the dark. I concluded that the shadow in my far sight was just an illusion. Until I was blindsided by a black body in a hoodie.
I reached for my phone.
It struck again.

On the ground.
Bleeding out.
Blinded by the blood in my eye.
Stubborn, and filled with too much pride.

The faceless figure approached nearer.
The faint whispers became clear.

I told him:
"I was bred to not stay down without a fight. If you want what I got, you have to be ready to die."

He responded:
"Silly child, I desire not your meager tangibles.
I want your life.

Change your course. Rid yourself of your worthless gold. Submit your soul onto the Lord or perish with your worldly possessions.

It is up to you."

"Open My Heart" by Yolanda Adams

What are your thoughts?

I pray to the Lord my soul to take

Thought: Remember Me

I learned not to think much of how this book is judged by the cover

Just do not let it get into me

Wearing my heart on my sleeve

Bumping shoulders with my enemies

Lately

They have been closer than my friends

Depending on social media for updates about major life events

Lately

Dear moments been turning into distant memories

Lately

It has been hard fighting this need not to feel lonely

Winters been getting colder

Consuming *Coco*

Contemplating if "they gon' remember me"

"Remember Me" on Coco Soundtrack
(Best Disney animated film of all time)
"Farewell" by J. Cole

Photo by Stephen Ezekoye

I am Derick Stephenson Jr. I am originally from Jacksonville, FL. That city is the burial ground for many of my darkest secrets. Simultaneously, it is a haven for some of my fondest memories.

    I really do not think of myself as anyone special. I know that I breathe like you breathe. I bleed like you bleed. I remember a period in my life when people would ask me what I wanted to be. I told them I wanted to be a good person. Never really wanted to make it big. Wherever I go, whatever my future holds, I just want to make a difference.

@JustDaMessenger
Justdamessenger.com

"Real Person" by Caleborate

The End!

Thought: No Edit

Some would call this a true stream of consciousness. Where you kind of just let your thoughts flow. Type as you go. In school we use to call it a brain dump. You would not really worry about editing. The goal was to generate thought and write everything that comes to mind. I wonder what it would be like to just release a book of my brain dumps. I probably could not do that because folks are so judgmental. I'd be too worried about their judgment. I would say that I have learned to act. I have learned to be willing to put myself out there. It makes me think about my grandpa. I had a few folks in my life that I considered to be like grandparents. For a while, I did not have a strong connection with any of my biological grandparents. Some point in high school I got connected with one of my grandpas. I still hadn't seen him in years, but we talked over the phone a lot. Time went on. I was in college. He called me to check in on my progress. I figured I'd send him a copy of my transcript. I also wrote him a personal letter. I put it in the envelope and had it ready to mail off. Someone gave me the idea to put a picture in it considering that he had not seen me in a while. I figure it was a good thought. Issue is that I never did it. Literally a week following, he passed away. That was September 27th, 2013. I held on to that letter up until the house fire. It was a reminder that some things can't be edited. I encourage you to act now. Go after it. Do not leave a page unwritten.

If no one else tells you this today, you're loved and appreciated.

www.ingramcontent.com/pod-product-compliance
Lightning Source LLC
Chambersburg PA
CBHW031504040426
42444CB00007B/1201